Narcissistic Abuse Recovery

A Guide To Finding Clarity And Reclaiming Your Joy After Leaving A Toxic Relationship

© Copyright 2018 - All rights reserved.

The content contained within this book may not be reproduced, duplicated or transmitted without direct written permission from the author or the publisher.

Under no circumstances will any blame or legal responsibility be held against the publisher, or author, for any damages, reparation, or monetary loss due to the information contained within this book. Either directly or indirectly.

Legal Notice:

This book is copyright protected. This book is only for personal use. You cannot amend, distribute, sell, use, quote or paraphrase any part, or the content within this book, without the consent of the author or publisher.

Disclaimer Notice:

Please note the information contained within this document is for educational and entertainment purposes only. All effort has been executed to present accurate, up to date, and reliable, complete information. No warranties of any kind are declared or implied. Readers acknowledge that the author is not engaging in the rendering of legal, financial, medical or professional advice. The content within this book has been derived from various sources. Please consult a licensed professional before attempting any techniques outlined in this book.

By reading this document, the reader agrees that under no circumstances are is the author responsible for any losses, direct or indirect, which are incurred as a result of the use of information contained within this document, including, but not limited to, —errors, omissions, or inaccuracies.

CONTENTS

Introduction 9
Chapter One: Narcissistic Abuse 12
    Who is a Narcissist? 13
    Are You a Narcissist, or Do You
    Know One? 14
        Dimension 1: One-Sided Listening 15
        Dimension 2: Always ME 15
        Dimension 3: Rules are Only for Others ... 16
        Dimension 4: Don't You Dare to
        Criticize Me 16
        Dimension 5: It is Your Fault 16
        Dimension 6: I Am Always Angry
        Because You Make Me Angry 17
    What is Narcissistic Abuse? 18
        Verbal Abuse 18
        Covert Aggression 18
        Emotional Blackmail 19
        Gaslighting 19
        Hovering 20
        Baiting 20

- *Crossing the Boundaries* 21
- *Defaming your Character* 21
- *Physical Violence* 21
- *Isolation* 21

Types of Narcissist 22

- *Exhibitionist Narcissists* 23
- *Closet Narcissists* 23
- *Toxic Narcissists* 25

Daily Meditations day 1-5 26

Chapter Two: How to Avoid the Trap and Get Going? 32

How Do You Handle Narcissist Abuse? 34

Stages of Recovery 38

- *First Stage – The VICTIM* 38
- *Second Stage – The SURVIVOR* 40
- *Third Stage – The SURTHRIVER* 42

Daily Meditations Day 6-10 43

Chapter Three: The Road to Recovery 50

Practical Difficulties 51

The Road to Recovery 54

Experience Solitude 55
Therapist 55
Practice Meditation 56

Chapter Four: Why Recovering can be Hard? ... 63

Love Patterns of a Narcissist 64

I Miss Him Badly – What Do I Do Now? ... 67

Strategies to Move On 70

Let Truth be Your Best Friend 70
Practice Mindfulness 70
Heal Yourself by Reconnecting 71

Chapter Five: Don't Fall for a Narcissist Again 79

How Do You Save Yourself from the Radar of a Narcissist? 80

Conclusion 91

Sources 92

Introduction

I would like to take this opportunity to thank you for purchasing this book, *"Narcissistic Abuse Recovery."*

The ideal image a narcissist portrays about himself is that he loves and respects others; however, that is not true. In fact, narcissists don't love themselves. Narcissists are driven by shame, and deep down they can differentiate between their pretense (the image they show the world) and their actual self (shame-based). They try too hard to suppress the shame they feel by using negative defense mechanisms that ultimately destroy relationships by causing pain and permanent damage to their loved ones.

The coping mechanisms used by most narcissists are extremely abusive, and it is for this reason that the term narcissistic abuse is used; however, not all the people who abuse are narcissists. For example, people suffering from borderline personality disorders, bipolar disorder and anti-social personality disorder (sociopaths) can also be abusive. Addicts also fall under this category. Regardless of what the diagnosis of an abuser is, it cannot be denied that abuse is abuse.

If you are a victim of abuse, you must challenge yourself by:

- Identifying the abuse.
- Getting help at the right time and building a favorable support system.
- Working on how to protect yourself and growing stronger.

Narcissistic abuse can potentially ruin you by:

- Forcing you to withdraw.
- Sucking the soul out of you.
- Making you abandon your individuality.
- Shattering you into pieces with the dangerous consequences.

If you suffer from narcissistic abuse, you will start to hate yourself and develop a sense of worthlessness that may want you to end your life. Narcissistic abuse can affect your willpower and affect your mental and physical strength. You keep revisiting the horrors and may decide that the abuse is never going to end leaving you powerless, but, a little support and interference can make a huge difference. Don't hesitate to ask for help.

This book will serve as an effective guide and help you recover from narcissistic abuse. Over the course of the book, you will gather information on what narcissistic abuse is, how to identify if you are being abused, and the road to recovery from the abuse. You will also learn to protect yourself from narcissistic abuse and learn to fight back.

I hope this book serves as an informative and interesting read to you. This book provides the basic information about narcissistic abuse, however what makes it unique is that it includes a 30 day plan with nuggets that help every stage of the recovery process. Some part of this process is going to be extremely painful, as you confront the truth of what you were subjected to. This is the reason why I included a guide for studying the bible and using prayers through this process. Like most people who have gone through this have shared, meditation and prayers are invaluable tools for emotional healing.

Chapter One: Narcissistic Abuse

An individual is capable of abusing or hurting another person when he or she is hurt or angry. The difference between a narcissist and any other individual is the guilt. When you control, judge, withhold or criticize others (loved ones or anyone in general), you tend to feel guilty at some point in time, often when your anger or frustration subside. In the case of a narcissist, they never feel guilty about their actions.

The abuse of a narcissist can be:

- Emotional
- Physical
- Financial
- Sexual
- Mental or/and
- Spiritual

Narcissistic abuse is often emotional, and it is

difficult for most individuals to identify that they are being abused. Manipulation, emotional threats and psychological intimidation are used to exercise control over you, which ultimately results in mental torture. They are experts in verbal abuse and manipulation, and they know how to push you to a state where you begin to doubt your own sanity.

Who is a Narcissist?

These people usually appear fun to be with since they present themselves as compassionate and loving personalities. Everybody would want to be friends or surround themselves with such people, and there are times when the relationship could become romantic. Narcissists are often deemed as the ideal choices for partners. You will love hanging around with them, but do you think they can be good partners?

Do you have a friend or are you in a relationship with someone who only loves talking about himself or herself? Were you shocked when they first snapped at you for talking about your problems? Did the person make you feel like your pain or struggle is nothing compared to what they have been through or are going through? Did they intentionally change the topic when you were explaining something of utmost importance?

A listening disorder is one of the main things you will come across with a narcissist. When you rewind it all, you will realize that you were doing the listening most of the time. It is quite difficult to maintain friendship with such an individual, It is difficult to talk to someone who does not want to hear you out or is quick to dismiss anything you say. However, the narcissist is very charming in the beginning of a romantic relationship. They would make you feel so special to the point of idolizing you, they tell you things like you are better than all the people they had ever been with. Their motive is to draw you in, eventually the abuse would start.

Are You a Narcissist, or Do You Know One?

Taking this simple quiz can help you answer the above question. There are six dimensions to assess whether or not a person is narcissistic. Give yourself, or the person you know, the score for each dimension from 0 to 5 (zero=no narcissism; 5=always).

It will be good if you can first assess yourself before you assess the person who you think might be a narcissist. It is best to do this to ensure that you are not a narcissist before you judge another person. You can identify your own patterns, as well as the other person's patterns more clearly than ever by answering the following questions:

Dimension 1: One-Sided Listening

What I need to say and what I want is all that matters when I converse with others. The decisions made are dependent only on my concerns and feelings. Another person's emotions are not relevant to me and it does not affect me. My opinions are always right when it comes to discussing issues or problems. Another person's opinion doesn't really matter because it is wrong and is not of great importance to me. If my opinions are questioned, my intentions are under scrutiny.

Dimension 2: Always ME

I have better and interesting information, and always have a lot to say about how I feel and what I have achieved. I do not have the time to listen to another person since their achievements do not matter as much. If there is something I want, I must get it immediately. I do not worry or care about another person's emotions because they do not concern me.

Dimension 3: Rules are Only for Others

It is always my way or the highway. Rules do not apply to me. I am allowed to have relationships, but my friend does not have that right.

Dimension 4: Don't You Dare to Criticize Me

If another person is concerned about my wellbeing or intentions, he or she is indirectly criticizing my actions. It hurts when I am criticized, but I am allowed to do it because I am right; however, if another person does it, they hurt me and I will do anything to get back at them. I often feel I am blamed for being myself. These actions and thoughts are clinically termed as *'Personalizing the criticism.'* For example, if you tell a narcissist that you miss them, they often take it as an accusation. They may ask you if you feel that they do not spend enough time with you.

Dimension 5: It is Your Fault

If things do not work out between us, it is never my fault because I am always right. I cannot be blamed and the other person should never expect me to apologize. If my faults and issues are brought out and the other person mentions how those faults affected the relationship, I will get mad at you because I cannot be criticized.

Dimension 6: I Am Always Angry Because You Make Me Angry

My anger flares because of the other person. If they do not listen to me or constantly criticize me, I will get mad. I will never apologize because I have done nothing wrong. I can give the other person a million examples of where they went wrong so they should apologize to me.

Have you calculated your score? If your score is less than, or equal to 10, you do not have to worry since you are healthy. If your score is more than 10, then your habits resonate narcissism. Do not panic, but pay attention to the dimensions and try to work on them. When you have identified the dimensions you need to work on, you can become less of a narcissist.

A score greater than 18 is really serious and you must take active steps to work on your narcissistic habits and eliminate those that don't serve you well. If your score is greater than 24, it indicates that you need to work on your personal growth. Get some professional help and work on your habits.

What is Narcissistic Abuse?

As mentioned earlier, narcissistic abuse may be physical, emotional, sexual, mental or spiritual.

Verbal Abuse

Not all verbal abuse can be tagged as narcissistic. You must look at the context, frequency and the spite (hatred/vengeance) in the behavior since people often criticize, interrupt, blame, be sarcastic, oppose, block or blame you depending on what the situation may be. You must assess the frequency of this behavior. Bullying, name calling, shaming, belittling, demanding, blaming, threatening, criticizing, getting violent, accusing, undermining and ordering are all verbal abuse.

Covert Aggression

Indirectly influencing you to behave in a manner that befits the goals of the narcissist is called manipulation. You aren't verbally abused, but you are manipulated by their harmless or sweet words. Their action or words may seem to compliment you, but at a subconscious level you know you are hurt. It isn't easy to recognize this type of behavior and you often brush it off since you believe he or she loves you.

Emotional Blackmail

Emotional blackmail is common in most relationships these days. People have learnt the art of using sensitive statements or emotions to make their partner think that their partner was wrong. Emotional blackmail is another form of manipulation and may include punishment, anger, threats, intimidation or warning.

Gaslighting

Gaslighting is a technique used by people with personality disorders such as narcissist, to manipulate and control others. Gaslighting tactics include changing the facts of events and sometimes even denying that they ever occurred, they insist that their victims imagine things and often call them crazy. The goal here is to make the victim question their own memory, and sanity. The victim often feels helpless and begins to question his or her judgment leading them to believe that they are incompetent. They become fully dependent on the narcissist. A narcissist uses this method since it is one of the best weapons in their arsenal.

Hovering

A narcissist uses this approach to rekindle the relationship with the victim if the victim has chosen to leave them, or has turned a deaf ear to their conversations. Often, narcissists declare their undying and unconditional love for their partner by saying that they cannot move on without them. For instance, when the partner says, "I am madly in love with you. I have never felt this way before. It was only after you left I realized how much I missed you. I need you back. I am sorry. I cannot live another moment without you. Please come back," the victim gets emotional and starts to rethink his or her decision. Since love is a powerful emotion, narcissists don't fail to use it to achieve their goals.

Baiting

A narcissist baits his or her victim by pushing them over the edge to elicit an extreme emotion from them. They often taunt the victim, causing the victim to break down psychologically and emotionally. Narcissists find this fun since they love watching their victims suffer.

Crossing the Boundaries

When someone invades your personal space, it can either lead to anger if you are mentally strong to resist or to a sense of helplessness if you are weak. Checking your mailbox, reading through your phone messages, stalking your social profiles, physically following you, denying your privacy, etc. all fall under this category.

Defaming your Character

Narcissists often spread lies about you or begin nasty rumors about you that could tarnish your reputation. This approach destroys the victim emotionally.

Physical Violence

Hitting you, throwing stuff at you, destroying your things, pulling your hair, sexually exploiting you, etc. all comes under this category.

Isolation

The narcissist will isolate you from the outside world (family, friends or social gatherings). They use verbal abuse, physical control, character assassination or emotional blackmail to achieve this.

The severity of narcissistic abuse ranges from

physical to emotional – it can be violent aggression or being careless about your emotions or feelings. Although most narcissists don't feel guilty and often play the blame game, there are some who are capable of accepting the guilt when they begin to reflect on their actions.

Types of Narcissist

Narcissists are classified into three categories:

- Exhibitionist narcissists (these people expect to be admired)
- Closet narcissists (would like to cling on to people they admire)
- Toxic narcissists (domineering)

Theorists may come up with different names for them, or classify them into more or fewer categories. For instance, some may classify both toxic and closet narcissists as covert narcissists, or may refer to toxic narcissists as malignant narcissists. The behavior or quality of the narcissist defines the type. People who exhibit extreme qualities of narcissism are referred to as narcissists and are said to have a narcissistic personality disorder.

Exhibitionist Narcissists

These people will always want to be the center of attention – they seek admiration and often get dominant during conversations by telling stories, and sharing their experiences, etc. They expect to be treated specially and love giving advice, regardless of whether or not they are asked for it. They shift into the GOD (Grandiose, Omnipotent, and Devaluing) mode whenever they feel insecure to defend their values and opinions. Simply put, this type of narcissist develops an unrealistic pretense to hide their self-doubt. They present themselves as being perfect. They fail to understand that a human being cannot be perfect.

What would be their relationship style? These people tend to be too bossy and are completely insensitive to others' emotions. They expect their partner to agree with them on anything and everything - as well as admire them immensely. The moment you disagree with them, you are perceived as someone who constantly criticizes them. They must constantly be reassured that they are the perfect partner.

Closet Narcissists

Closet narcissists don't prefer to be the center of

attention. They do like to be treated specially, but they do not like the attractions that most exhibitionists like. This may be because they were taught that being open for admiration might lead to attacks. Psychologists feel that these people may be brought up that way as their own parents may have been exhibitionists and they look at their children as their competitors. The parents devalued them and showered them with praises or rewards while complimenting themselves. The narcissistic ostentation is the foundation of their personality, which ultimately results in the development of an inferiority complex. They are vulnerable or exposed when they are the center of attraction. They fear that they would be attacked for their flaws.

They would compromise this by associating themselves with people whom they admire and then feel special because of this association. They don't demand openly, but get things done indirectly by playing the victim card. Pity is their weapon. They act like they are really nice but, in reality, they aren't. They use the victim card to convince you to do what they want. Most of these people also allow themselves to be used by their friends. They want to be praised for the effort and hard work they put in to get things done for the people they admire.

What would be their relationship style? Their choice would be a special ideal partner. They feel relaxed with the brilliance of their partner. They follow the Midas touch formula. They believe that they are special or worthy of admiration when they associate themselves with someone who is admired by people. These people often get into a relationship with exhibitionists since they believe that the defense mechanism of an exhibitionist is confidence.

Toxic Narcissists

The meanest people of the narcissist group are the toxic narcissists. They are extremely dominative and want others to submit themselves. They display a sadistic approach and enjoy hurting people. They feed on your fear and envy anyone who has achieved things they weren't able to achieve. They often live with dreams of unrealistic fantasies. You can see your irritating sweet old aunt in them, as they love embarrassing you in public.

What would be their relationship style? They will always make you feel worthless and inferior to them. They wouldn't hesitate to go that extra mile to pull you down and, no matter what you do, you can never please them. Your self-confidence will be replaced with self-doubt.

Daily Meditations day 1-5
Day 1: You are not alone

You have been through the fire, beaten down physically, mentally and emotionally. Take solace in this truth, you are not alone. It is unimaginable to be stripped bare of your dignity, the first days are usually the most difficult, the confusion and pain. Meditating on the scriptures has been extremely effective for victims of emotional abuse. Today we are looking at Psalm 91:4 and psalm 91 is one of the most uplifting scriptures.

Psalm 91:4

He shall cover thee with his feathers, and under his wings shalt thou trust: his truth shall be thy shield and buckler

What ever you have lost, you are alive and even though in pain, the Lord promises us in this verse of his everlasting love that is never going to change. Read the whole of psalm 91 and meditate on all the verses that expound on how the lord has promised to care for you.

Prayer: Lord, I don't know how I am going to survive this, I feel empty. I don't know who I am anymore, I feel lost and afraid. But, I believe in your undying love for me. I know with your help I am going to survive and thrive.

DAY 2: Confusion is normal

Leaving an abusive relationship leaves the victim feeling confused. Whether you find yourself asking why you put up with the abuse for so long, or why you were treated so badly by someone who you loved, there are some questions that would never get answered. Turning to the abuser to gain clarity is most likely going to cause more harm to you. Remember recovery is not going to happen suddenly or easily, it is a journey you would have to go on for yourself, to get back all that was taken from you. When you feel overwhelmed with confusion, rest the fact that God has promised, everything is going to be okay.

John 16:33

These things I have spoken to you, that in me ye might have peace. In the world ye shall have tribulation: but be of good cheer; I have overcome the world.

Day 3: It's a wound non the less

Emotional abuse is also referred to as hidden abuse just because it leaves scares that are internal. Acknowledge the fact that you have been wounded non the less, and the lord cares about your healing. In him there is no shame, no blaming. His love is pure, and he loves you just the way you are in this moment. In your weakness is his strength made perfect in you. Be naked and unashamed in your prayers. Those things you feel so ashamed about, too ashamed to tell even those closest to you. Talk to him about it. I would suggest using journaling to prayerfully go through your emotions.

Write down exactly how you feel, and search into the scriptures to also write down what the lord has said concerning you. One thing is sure, you might be wounded but you are a survivor, you are still here and God is not done with you yet.

Psalm 147:3

He healeth the broken in heart, and bindeth up their wounds

Your broken heart would be mended, trust that the lord who knows it all would fix all the wounded parts of your life. Your self confidence, your emotional and mental health, your mind, your physical body, and your relationships.

Day 4: Blame can only pull you backward

Chances are you were a target for a narcissist because of your compassionate nature and ability to empathize. No one is perfect and in no way is having empathy a bad thing. Blaming yourself for the abuse is not going to help move you forward for healing. Relationships have problems, because again we are all imperfect beings. The need you have for love is not a bad thing, you cannot blame yourself for wanting to be loved. Did your friends and family warn you about your abuser and instead of making the decision for you, you choose to cover for your abusive partner instead? and now you blame yourself for being sucked back into the relationship over and over again.

There are many complexities about the abuse you may never understand. I urge you to put the things that are in the past behind you.

Philippians 3:13

Of course, my friends, I really do not think that I have already won it; the one thing I do, however, is to forget what is behind me and do my best to reach what is ahead.

Pray for Gods helping in putting the past where it belongs, behind you.

Day 5: One day at a time

You might be struggling with keeping low contact or no contact with your ex. You are curious to know if they miss you, what they are up to, who they are with. A good strategy would be to unfollow them from social media if you were both active there, and also avoid those mutual friends who might assist them in pulling you back in or even remind you of them.

If you find yourself just going through the motions of your day, being absent minded for the most part, remind yourself that you have survived. It would take as long as it takes to heal, and you would be stronger for it.

1 Peter 5: 10

But after you have suffered for a little while, the God of all grace, who calls you to share his eternal glory in union with Christ, will himself perfect you and give you firmness, strength, and a sure foundation.

Suffering happens because we are imperfect and selfish, as humans we are flawed and unable to love the way God does. But his promises are yes and Amen. We can be sure God has no hidden agenda. Pray for his strength to see you through.

Chapter Two: How to Avoid the Trap and Get Going?

It is possible to avoid getting trapped or provoked by a narcissist when you are able to guess his or her motives. When you forget the abuser's intentions, you often react in the following ways:

- You may choose to pacify the abuser, avoid anger or conflicts. By doing this, you are indirectly giving the power to your abuser. He or she will look at your actions as a sign of weakness and seize the opportunity to exercise more control over you.

- You may plead with your abuser for many reasons. Never plead with your abuser as the narcissists look at it as a sign of weakness (which they loathe in themselves). They may dismiss you with deep disgust or disrespect you.

- You may want to withdraw yourself from your abuser, but this does not work well with a narcissist.

- You may want to present facts to them and argue with them; however, this will only drain your energy since they aren't really bothered by the facts. All they want is to justify they are right so when you argue or fight (by raising your voice) you only cause more damage to yourself.

- You may choose to deny the allegations laid on you and defend your actions, but you are indirectly approving the narcissist's stand to abuse or judge you. Simply denying is okay, but defending your actions is not going to work in your favor.

- You may try to make the abuser understand you better. This will not work in your favor since the narcissist will only show his or her superiority. It is best to avoid sharing your emotions with the narcissist as you only hurt yourself more. There are chances that he or she might even manipulate you further.

- You may criticize your abuser and worsen the situation since the abuser will only be provoked. A narcissist is insecure and weak at his or her core so they cannot take it when you complain.

- You may want to threaten the abuser, but do not do that unless you can implement that threat since there are chances it may backfire.

- You may excuse the abuser or rationalize with him or her. This action indirectly encourages the abuser to do what he or she is doing. The more you allow the abuse to happen, the weaker you become. You must remember that a narcissist seldom changes.

- You may want to blame yourself and change yourself to become the version of you that the abuser likes. Whatever you do, you can never please the narcissist, especially when his or her ultimate motive is only to abuse you and gain pleasure from your pain.

How Do You Handle Narcissist Abuse?

You must deal with your abuser effectively. If you continue to allow the abuse, you are deliberately damaging your self-esteem. You must confront the abuser by talking calmly and clearly. You shouldn't react, but respond. Fighting or arguing will only encourage him or her more, therefore, you need to respond calmly and set boundaries to shield your body, emotion and mind.

You need to be treated with respect and dignity. The narcissist abuser cannot take advantage of you by forcing you to do things that you aren't interested in. It is your right to privacy, your right to not be touched, your right to not have sex if you aren't interested, your right to have feelings and your right to not be shouted at. If you were once a victim (in childhood), your self-esteem would have already been tarnished, as you no longer trust yourself. In such cases, it is best to get support by meeting a therapist.

Don't get aggressive or withdraw from people; you need to be assertive in your responses. Maybe quick short-term responses will work well.

- It hurts when you criticize me often. Please stop. (Just walk away after saying this.)
- I can never be the husband (or wife) you wished for.
- Maybe that is your opinion but I don't

agree with it.

- You were saying that…repeat whatever he or she said and close the conversation with…hmm, I see.)
- I don't want to talk to you when you…(mention the abuse, for example - criticize me, and offend me, etc. after saying this, and just leave the place.)
- Alternatively, You can say something that will lighten the mood - "You know you look like a cute panda when you are angry."
- If you are accused of something that is true, then just agree to it. For instance, yes, you are right, I did burn the dinner. Say this and ignore the part where he had called you a bad cook or irresponsible.

Be clear in what you want and understand what your narcissist partner wants from you. Be aware of where you have power and use it effectively with the narcissist. Remember, you are dealing with a person who has a personality disorder and therefore, you will need to apply certain strategies to make things better.

If people mistreat you, it is because you are allowing them to do so. Your boundaries and rules decide how you allow people to treat you. Analyze yourself, know your rights, get in touch with your feelings, listen to your body and learn to be assertive. Be explicit. Don't give hints or expect them to read your mind.

If your boundaries are ignored, then you need to communicate and show the consequences. You are not threatening them but taking actions to shield yourself.

Educate yourself by conducting research on narcissism and identify the behavioral patterns. Understand that the narcissist has a neurological deficiency that affects their reactions. The best way to deal with them is to treat them like a child – explain the impact of their behavior and motivate them to change it by giving them incentives. Your communication should be neutral and not emotional.

It is often difficult to stand up against someone you love or had once loved. It requires support as you had already fallen prey to their abusive actions. You need to eliminate self-doubt and work on self-realization. Challenging a change to your own reaction is tough; therefore, it is necessary to seek help (maybe a supportive non-judgmental friend or a therapist).

Even if your narcissist partner doesn't change after all your attempts, you will at least be equipped with tools to shield yourself from further abuse. Your confidence and self-worth will grow.

Stages of Recovery

There are three stages of narcissistic abuse recovery:

- Victim
- Survivor
- Surthriver

First Stage – The VICTIM

As a victim, you might be going through a series of emotions and feelings like:

- Betrayal from the one you loved
- Being victimized by friends and family
- Humiliation
- Hurt

- Denial
- Uncertainty
- Feelings of rejection
- Rage

You may also accuse yourself for all that has happened:

- Angry at yourself for not understanding your partner earlier.
- Angry at yourself for the lost time – for all the love you gave him or her.
- Panic (financially and psychologically). In the case of having children, you may be worried about your plan of action.
- Scared about the future, although it has changed for the better.
- Fear of ending up alone forever.
- Being abandoned by your family and friends

What can you do to overcome this?

- Is your partner a narcissist? What are the signs you missed?

- Understand narcissist abuse.
- Dwell into details – check the behavioral patterns (you might end up discovering things you never knew, so be prepared to get shocked).
- Accept the reality and understand that you are not alone.
- Question yourself. What made you the victim? How did you become the target? Study more on narcissists and their victims.
- Find the answers to all your questions.
- Work on how to get away from the abusive relationship.

Second Stage – The SURVIVOR

Now that you have understood how you became a victim, you need to learn to survive.

How are you feeling now?

- Do you have trust issues?
- Do past events trigger fear or anger?
- Do you have trouble forgiving?
- Do you know how to care for yourself?

- Are you struggling to rebuild?
- Are you seeking professional help?
- Have you taken the time out to meet new people?

How prepared are you on the mental aspect?

- Are you working on self-soothing approaches?
- Are you confident and self-aware?
- Are you still depressed?
- Have you discovered what event in your childhood led to the situation?
- Are you hyperactive and constantly worried about meeting another narcissist?
- Are you restoring your finances?

What must you learn to overcome the post-abuse stress?

- Seek a therapist to heal your post-traumatic stress disorder (PTSD).
- Work harder to get back to your older self.
- Don't isolate yourself. Reconnect with your friends and family.

- Go out and enjoy.
- Continue to learn about narcissism and emotional abuse.
- Understand your vulnerability, feel the gratitude and experience happiness. Live the moment.
- If you find it difficult to forget and forgive, divert your concentration to things you love to do.

Third Stage – The SURTHRIVER

Are you still overcome by negative emotions?

- Are you resentful and angry with the one who did this to you?
- Does your past haunt you?
- Do you still carry the unresolved emotional baggage from your past?
- Are you embarrassed for having been a victim to your abuser?
- Are you ashamed that the narcissist used you?
- Is everything at a standstill?
- Do you find it difficult to get back to work

and rebuild your life?

Do you feel like you have not become the person you had wanted to be?

- Do you feel that you will never be able to forgive your abuser, or rather don't want to forgive him or her?
- Do you think others judge you for not creating your own life and moving on?
- Do you yearn for true freedom – to do things you once loved to do?
- Do you want to pursue your passionate dream?

How do you learn to overcome this?

Daily Meditations Day 6-10
Day 6: It is time to let go.

You need to refocus on your life. You need to understand how dangerous it is to hold onto emotional attachments from the past. When you break free from a narcissist, you bring your old self back and venture into creating a new life. Its time to let go of the good bad and ugly parts of being with a narcissist, and view this experience as an opportunity to do all the things in life you always wanted to do. Like a new beginning, a fresh start. Give yourself the closure you desperately seek by understanding everything this book has taught about this mental disorder. You have to be okay with the fact that your ex-partner is not going to change, they do not have what it takes to give you the love you deserve.

1 Peter 5:7

Leave all your worries with him, because he cares for you.

Prayer: Father, I don't have the power on my own to overcome this hurt and pain. Please help me. I let go of every evil that was done to me, I ask for your healing for my mind body and soul. I cast all my worries on you. I want to begin a new chapter and leave all this behind. Supply me with your peace that passes understanding and make me whole again.

Day 7: Love yourself.

Be confident about your worth. Self-confidence is the motivational energy that can push you forward. When you practice self-love, you are no longer chaotic, overwhelmed or anxious but, instead, you learn to be calm, work on options and bring joy to oneself. Think about some of the things you did in the past that gave you a confidence boost. Those things you were good at before the abuse started and caused you to doubt yourself. Learn all over again to prioritize your well being and happiness. Self love is about accepting ourselves, with all our flaws. Self love is more than a pampering session at the spa, its more about our internal conversations, how kind we are to ourselves.

Ephesians 5:29

None of us ever hate our own bodies. Instead, we feed them, and take care of them, just as Christ does the church

Prayer: Lord, help me to see myself through your loving eyes. That when I was still in sin, you sent your son to die for me. Help me to be kind to myself, so I can fully embrace the essence of who you have created me to be

Day 8: Be present in the moment.

Work on mindfulness – get rid of the anxiety and bring calmness to your mind and soul. Enjoy the simple moments – watch a bird fly, feel the wind on your face, play with your cat, go trekking, and explore new places. Get adventurous and be curious to learn new things. Make peace with your past, nothing you do now can change it. There is so much value you bring to the world. Focus on ways you can contribute to others, this helps to build a renewed zest for life, it is very uplifting too. Work towards increasing your self awareness, by questioning limiting ideas.

Esther 4:14b

Yet who knows—maybe it was for a time like this that you were made queen

Prayer: Father, I cannot keep asking why this happened to me. I ask that you turn around this situation to work for your glory and for my good. I don't know how that is going to happen right now, but I ask that you use my story, my pain to be a source of healing to someone else.

Day 9: Be open to new experiences.

Connect to more positive and authentic relationships – be it friends or acquaintances. Let your relationship be healthy and get rid of anxiety, stress, fear and unnecessary triggers. Understand that not everyone is out to harm you, watch out for excessive defensiveness. Do not self sabotage new relationships. As you progress in your healing journey, you would be able to set healthy boundaries for new relationships, your confidence and self awareness would also attract healthier people into your life. Through this experience you have discovered who your true friends were, those who stood by you, supporting you financially and many other ways. Many have left your life and that's okay too. Quality and not quantity is desirable in friendships.

1 Corinthians 13:3

I may give away everything I have, and even give up my body to be burned, but if I have no love, this does me no good.

Prayer: Father, I don't trust myself to make the right decisions in relationships, so I pray that you order my steps and divinely connect me with the right people who would help me grow, even as I also add immense value to them. Renew my faith in Love and in people. Thank you for the friends, family and/or people you have brought into my life who have been of tremendous help in my healing, bless them and meet them always at the point of their need.

Day 10: Stop recounting your past horrors.

Don't feel guilty and harp on how things could have been different if only you had done this or that (erase the if-only in your life). Accept that you were a victim and pat yourself on the back that you survived it. Avoid going into conversations that take you back to start analyzing details of the abuse. Repeating those scenarios would surely lead to depression. When you find your mind drifting to despair, stop it immediately by verbally expressing gratitude for where you are. Yes! Say it out loud. Gratitude is a good weapon against negative emotions, they do not cohabit. If you around you, there is something to be thankful for.

Jeremiah 29:11 (GNT)

I alone know the plans I have for you, plans to bring you prosperity and not disaster, plans to bring about the future you hope for.

Prayer: Father, empower me to focus on your love for me, and your promises. I take all of my doubts, and I lay them at your feet. Fill my heart with your word, and let it take over every negative habit of recounting the evil I endured. Father those things that are true, and filled with virtue, let me think on those as I take a step closer towards recovery.

Chapter Three: The Road to Recovery

It is true that you were a victim, but rehashing the events of the past does not help you recover. When you do this, you unconsciously give a chance for negativity to control you. Your experiences should shape you and not define who you are. You can create a new and powerful identity from them. Instead of perceiving yourself as a victim, identify yourself as a target since it is easy for anybody to become a target. Unfortunately, you were under the radar of a narcissist but what next?

Now that you know the dangerous effects of narcissism and how harmful it can be to your life, you have a choice to decide on what to do next. Rather than let your past ruin your future, you can use the experience to rewrite a new future. Don't be a victim without power but, in its place, be a target that turns down any form of manipulation.

Practical Difficulties

Getting trapped in a relationship with a narcissist is the toughest thing one can go through. Thirty-six-year-old Jocelyn shares her experience on how difficult she found it to get out of the trap:

"Get over this? How do you get over this? He courted me, wooed me and told my widowed mother that she'd never have to worry about me again. We said our vows at a wedding he paid for. I didn't notice that he had to control every detail including my dress and my weight. It was clear in no time. I tried and tried but the control was awful. Six years in, no kids, and I wanted out and he went insane. He sent the Elders of my church 'proof' that I was a whore, but he was the one cheating. It took two wasted years and tons of money I didn't have to get rid of him. How does anyone trust after this?"

It is often difficult to trust again since the person you loved and trusted the most betrayed you. The worst part is – letting go. Forty-two-year-old Lee found it really difficult to let go of his bitter past. He recounts that he had given her enough time to be reasonable and had, in fact, asked his lawyer to wait, but everything was in vain. After all these years, he is still angry with himself for the wasted time and money.

"I know it's not good for me to hold on to this experience, but I just can't let it go, you know?" – He says.

People who have been in a relationship with a narcissist will have similar feelings and thoughts about their ex-partners. Recovering from intimate relationships is always a difficult task – especially if it had been for a long time. Divorce after years of marriage can cause emotional turmoil to the person. When you realize that the person you thought you had known for years isn't exactly who he was, it can hurt you beyond words. Infidelity or any form of betrayal can add to the pain. He has been accusing you, making you feel guilty but, all the while, he has been doing things behind your back.

Most narcissists don't let go of their victims so easily – they try their best to bring them back to their life either to abuse or taunt. The author of 'Rethinking Narcissism,' Dr. Craig Malkin, mentions why it is tough to get over a relationship with a narcissist:

"People with Narcissistic Personality Disorder (NPD)

are often trapped in a constant battle between wanting you and pushing you away. Post break-up, that means they'll insinuate themselves back into your life, even if it's just to fire off an insulting text message ("You need your head examined.") or ask an infuriating question ("What did I do that was so bad?"). It takes two people to end a relationship, and many narcissists refuse to leave without a fight. Translation? Continued re-traumatization. It's no wonder so many of my clients panic when they see an email from their ex."

The emotional recovery after you separate from your narcissist partner can be a long journey, especially if you have kids who are really small. One of the doctor's client who is the mother of two (now grown-up children) had written to him,

"*I was married for five years and I have been divorced almost 12 years. The divorce has been ongoing in the sense that after finalization he has tormented my children and me for the past 12 years. I have been through two custody battles and endless amounts of money. I could go on and on. Yes, I do blame myself for being so stupid. I realized almost immediately after the wedding. Yes, I am angry. He has made my life a living hell. I've been working on dealing with him for years. I have a great therapist. No, I haven't been able to move on because, as long as the kids are under 18, I have to deal with evil. There is no truth to the statement that the abuse will stop after the divorce. The only difference is that he is not living in my house."*

The Road to Recovery

It can be a long and painful journey but you will have to fight without giving up hope. This is because the narcissist captures your most powerful asset – space (physical, emotional and psychological).

You will need physical space to feel free, emotional space to connect within yourself and psychological space to make sensible choices. The narcissist takes away all these from you which ultimately lead to self-doubt, fear and worthlessness. Your identity is reprogrammed and you are stolen of your individuality. You feel something is consuming you from the inside and you are emotionally exhausted.

You will now need to re-create this space and pick up all the broken pieces. You need to become the old you. Space can be personal or physical. How do you do this?

Experience Solitude

Take time out for yourself. Go to the nearby park and take a walk, visit your favorite café and have a cup of coffee, read a book sitting in your preferred spot, or go to the church where you can sit in peace and think. When you retreat, you give yourself enough time to think, feel and define your emotions. Solitude can help you see yourself, which can sometimes be a harsh experience but a much-needed one. You get a chance to reset, recreate and remember who you really are.

Therapist

Your therapist can be your aid who will allow you to explore your doubts and emotions. It is the safest space where you get to see yourself with an objective mirror and uncover your deepest fears. You get back to reality and understand that the narcissist had basically wanted to destroy your sanity in all ways. The power of therapy is such that it challenges you to fill all the gaps in your mind by allowing the emotions to flow in but, at the same time, gives you the true insights.

When you have recently ended an abusive relationship, you tend to get caught in illusion and fantasy. The therapist will challenge your illusions gently and encourage you to take responsibility for your life as well as your emotions. The damage caused by a narcissist is more than what you think – your thought pattern was reprogrammed, they created a set of beliefs within you, your confidence was shattered, your self-doubt grew and you were made to think that you are not good enough for them. The effect of all these lingers on within you even after the relationship is over. Taking the help of a therapist is the best way to reset your system and bring you back on track.

Practice Meditation

It can be quite impossible to meditate when your head is filled with so many thoughts and emotions. Try to practice meditation for a while. Go to your safe place, take a deep breath and focus on your body. Give it 10 to 15 seconds. Repeat whenever possible and slowly increase your time frame. Your mind will overcome you by replaying all your past bitter experiences, and your thoughts will flow beyond imagination, but be patient. Have the courage to bring yourself back to the present. You can find your peace when you practice meditation.

You will be completely separated from your mind

and meditation can help you reconnect back. Your mind is the target object for the narcissist – they will try to play with it by manipulating you, and they will exert control over you, but you need to avoid this. If not, you become vulnerable again to their attempts of getting back at you. Mindfulness increases awareness that gives you the power to fight the abuse.

You need to be firm in your practice sessions when you are recovering from a narcissistic abuse. You need to create a structural pattern and follow it. Get rid of the victim tag, create your own space, identify your obstacles and remind yourself that you are working to get better.

Day 11: No one can share your bitterness

It takes wisdom to take responsibility for our emotional wellbeing. As human beings, we tend to look outwardly, to either possessions or other people to make us happy. However, possessions can never fill a void in our lives. The moment the initial excitement wears off; we start seeking the next best thing to go after.

It is the the same way with relationships. No human being and complete you, or fill you. That is something only God can do. A great relationship can offer you an environment to love and be loved. When it come to your emotional health, you have to take responsibility moving forward. Make a decision to be Joyful, and grateful at all cost.

Your joy is your own; your bitterness is your own. No one can share them with you.

Proverbs 14:10

Prayer:

I cannot depend on things are people to complete me, whether I like to admit it or not. You are my source. Help me to let go of the bitterness, and fill my heart with your peace that passes all understanding.

Day12: Grant me courage

Fear can be so intense that it cripples survivors form moving forward in their lives. Most of the things you worry about are never going to materialize, yet they seem so real to you.

Mark Twain said, I am an old man, and have known a great many troubles, but most of them never happened.

Worry can be useful in the sense that you take

Narcissistic Abuse Recovery

precaution to protect yourself physically, or seek for help. However, allowing fear to become a dominant emotion in your life can become extremely toxic. What this means is that you are living like someone who has already been defeated before the fight has even begun.

Take back control of your mind, God is stronger than any enemy you will ever face.

But you, O LORD, are always my shield from danger; you give me victory and restore my courage.

Psalms 3:3

Prayer: Father, you have promised to restore my courage, I believe your word, I know that you are on my side, and I accept the report you have given concerning my situation. I have the victory. I am more than a conqueror.

Day13: What do you want?

Do you really want to get better? I this sounds like an odd question to be asking someone in pain. However, when someone has been in prolonged pain, it can be difficult to let go. To be completely free, you have to want that freedom, and freedom implies you have to let go. To let go of how this pain has defined you.

John 5:6

Jesus saw him lying there, and he knew that the man had been sick for such a long time; so he asked him, "Do you want to get well?"

Mark Buchanan commenting on this verse of scripture says "Sickness can actually steal the place of God, it can become a sick person's center, the touch stone by which he defines himself"

Prayer: Lord, I have held on to this pain for so long because it was the easiest thing to do. Help me to let go. Break down every wall that I have have built that keeps me captive to pain and open up new doors so I can find Joy again.

Day14: I am untouchable

Gods is all powerful, he determines the course of our lives. When he has made a promise to you, he would never break it. If you have lost material possessions as a part of the abuse, and you feel powerless about the situation, understand that you can get restoration of not just your health and emotions but of you finances too.

Hebrews 13:6

Let us be bold, then, and say, "The Lord is my helper; I will not be afraid. What can anyone do to me?"

Prayer: Lord, I know that I don't have to worry about my finances, cos you have promised to take care of me. Pleaser restore everything I have lost financially, show me all the ways I can fix the debt I am in, and send help to me.

Day15: Healed by his wounds

God can change your own heart; he can give you a new heart if you ask him. One that is able to love and to trust again. It doesn't matter how long you think you spent as a victim, you can start over again. You can be healed. Situations where you still have to deal with your ex for any reason (especially if there are kids involved) don't have to be painful. This can be difficult, but not impossible. Using strategies, you learn during therapy, and prayers as a the most important strategy you can disarm your abuser form getting to harm you.

Christ himself carried our sins in his body to the cross, so that we might die to sin and live for righteousness. It is by his wounds that you have been healed.

1 Peter 2:24

Prayer: Lord, I am healed. I refuse to be manipulated, or made to live in fear. Give me a new heart, one that is devoid of negativity and pain. I receive every good thing you have in store for me.

Chapter Four: Why Recovering can be Hard?

It can be extremely hard to recover from the trauma of narcissistic abuse as your belief in love and trust is contradicted. Your idea of honesty and loyalty has been tarnished and you no longer believe in it. Research confirms that divorce and break-ups are always agonizing, but coming out of a relationship with a narcissist is entirely different.

Recovery is not easy, but when you look into the intricacies, it should actually be easy for you to walk away from someone who had abused you emotionally, physically and psychologically. The person didn't respect you for who you are and therefore it should be easier to never turn back, but why doesn't it happen that way? Why is it harder to come out of an abusive relationship than it is to overcome a divorce or break-up? It is because you don't have the Casablanca effect. If you remember the scene in the movie Casablanca where the lead actress is asked to get on to the plane with her husband and she asks the lead actor – "What about us?" He says, "We'll always have Paris." The lead character is able to understand why she left him earlier and comes to terms with reality, yet he feels the pain of being abandoned but, he could regain the love and experience by revisiting their Paris moments.

Now, this is never going to happen with a narcissist because there was really no "We'll always have Paris" moment. Why is it so? Everything you ever believed in him, every connection, every promise, every moment spent together doesn't make any sense because you doubt if there was any reality in it. It is completely burned to ashes. When you walk away from a narcissist, you are not recovering from a failed relationship, but you are recuperating from warfare.

Love Patterns of a Narcissist

Did he ever love me – at least once? Will he be thinking about me now? Will he realize his mistake and come back to me? It is natural for you to ask these questions a hundred times in your head if you were truly and deeply in love with a narcissist. After all that he had done to you, you still have a faint hope somewhere in the corner of your heart that he will return to you.

It is not difficult to understand the patterns of these men and women, as they are quite predictable. Their relationship behavior is almost the same with all the people they have been with. It is easy for you to predict his behavior with you if you know their love pattern with their ex. This will give you more clarity as you begin to realize how they actually saw you, and if the relationship really meant anything at all to them.

Certain love patterns exhibited by the narcissist are so common that you can distinguish it by giving them names:

- The Hater
- The Romantic
- The Recycler
- The White Knight
- The Big Game Hunter
- The Novelty Seeker

Unfortunately, most women want their narcissist ex-partner if he displayed 'The Romantic' pattern often. Why is the loss so distressing for women that they long for him to come back? The fact is whatever your ex-partner had told you when he was in love with you was what he actually meant to say. Yes, you read it right. You are not crazy. He really meant it when he said he loved you.

He was in love with you – yes, he was in love with his idea of a perfect partner that he saw in you – a romantic fantasy of both as an ideal couple. The narcissist romantic loves the idea of a perfect romance – mesmerizing candlelight dinner, long car rides with you by his side, moonlight walks by the beach, perfect weekend getaways to a cozy cabin in the middle of the woods and the amazing passionate slow sex. His ultimate goal is to make every single moment romantic and intimate. He makes you feel that you are the most beautiful and loveable woman he has ever come across in his life. He makes it sound perfect by introducing you to his friends and social network as for how blessed he is to have you.

And then when you are so sure that you finally found your ideal partner and think about taking a step ahead, he backs off. You get to hear excuses on why he couldn't call you or meet you. You are confused and have no idea what is happening. Ignoring your emotions and feelings is the best weapon a narcissist will use to hurt you. If you were in a relationship with a normal guy, all these romantic moments and the passionate sex might have built a greater trust and led to genuine intimacy. In the case of narcissistic men, the moment they realize that the fantasy is becoming a reality, they go mute and start getting frustrated.

Some just walk away without paying heed to your emotions, while others torment you by breaking your confidence.

I Miss Him Badly – What Do I Do Now?

It is depressing to go through a break-up with a narcissist since it will test your patience and strength. You get thwarted by your own boundaries and all you feel is exhaustion – at all levels. You are unable to look at this as a relationship that is over as you yearn for the person to come back. Your grief and anger come bubbling at full speed, taking you away from reality. You expect things that are far from reality. You are overcome with mixed emotions where, at one point you want him, and the very next moment you never ever want to see his face in your life again. The feelings begin to get intense as it stretches from disgust to desire. Why does this happen?

The bond you had with the narcissist is traumatic, that you fail to see the difference between reality and fantasy. It is referred to as the trauma bond. The characteristic feature of trauma bond is you revisit your past so often that it takes up almost 100% of your brain energy resulting in controlling your nervous system not just for months, but for years together.

Your mind keeps churning all the memories that there comes a point where you fail to differentiate between the present and the past. Instead of being in the present, you get obsessed thinking if your ex-partner really cared for you, and if he is thinking about you at this very moment. You don't stop here - you go through a list of what-ifs in your head so that you soon lose yourself in the past.

Remember, a trauma bond is not love, but a form of emotional addiction. It takes you through a series of roller coaster rides that gives you the feeling of getting high. Confused? Often, the narcissistic partner abuses his victim with distressing arguments, spiteful insults and intensifies the fear of abandoning. Soon enough, this is followed by an extreme act of intimacy, soulful apologies and awesome sex.

So, when you think about the fights and arguments you had, instead of the agonizing pain, you end up thinking about the good moments that followed. You think he really cares or cared, but the truth is that was not love. Look at it from a third person's perspective; the moments you thought were breathtaking were actually not real. The feelings you are going through now – self-doubt, unworthiness, fear, etc were created by the narcissist.

When you continue to be in love with a narcissist, you are exposing yourself to more permanent damage. The trust, love and access you gave him allowed the virus to sneak into your system. Because of this, you are combating two viewpoints at a time – one is yours and the other is your ex-partner. Eventually, one of it has to die and you need to understand this. Disease and good health cannot co-exist.

Strategies to Move On

How do you do work on yourself and move on?

- Let truth be your best friend
- Practice mindfulness
- Heal yourself by reconnecting

Let Truth be Your Best Friend

Stop fantasizing and get back to reality. Make truth your best friend. Use a voice-recording app and record all the things you are able to recollect about your ex-partner (the abuses he hurled on you, the ways he tried to hurt you, etc). You can also write them down in a diary. Go through the list and summarize it into a list of points. Put it up in a place where you can see it regularly. Your last exercise will be to boil all the points down to a one-liner. For example, "The person is a leech who sucks my soul every time he enters my life, and I am in no mood to encourage him any further." Every time you are overcome by his thoughts, repeat the phrase to yourself.

Practice Mindfulness

You can break his spell and recuperate your attention by practicing mindfulness. It is impossible to wipe your thoughts completely but, instead, you can watch it from a neutral safe point. You don't allow the thoughts to consume you, but become an observer of your own mind who isn't judgmental.

Write down the list of things you would like to do for yourself – one or two things for a day. These can be simple things that help to nourish your soul and live in the moment. For instance, it can be walking your dog, preparing a meal, enjoying a spa massage, watching your favorite movie or doing yoga.

But remember, whatever you do, do it with all your heart. If your mind replays thoughts of your ex-partner, just repeat the one-liner you had written.

Heal Yourself by Reconnecting

After all that you had to go through, it is quite natural to want to stay away from people. You will need time for yourself – for your mind, soul and body. You need to click the reset button and start afresh. Trusting yourself will become difficult; forget trusting other people but tell yourself that it is okay and it is quite normal to go through such experiences.

Tell yourself that your intelligence has nothing to do with being victimized by a narcissist abuser. It was just bad luck that you fell into the hands of the perpetrator. The moment you realize this, you will find it easy to connect to yourself. All you wanted was to be loved, but things didn't go the way you expected it to. Give yourself some time to forget and forgive yourself.

Take a deep breath. Get to the analyzing mode. Be calm and begin to find an answer to the whys. This is needed so that you don't fall into the trap of a narcissist again. If you need to do this, you need to get connected to your inner self. Get out of the toxic environment and find a breathing place. Spend more time with animals and nature. Go dining with your trusted friends. Analyzing and over-thinking are completely two different things. You will be able to analyze only when your mind is clear and free of unwanted thoughts. Over-thinking is dangerous – you end up thinking about stuff that might not even happen. Go out for a movie, chat with your best friend, or plan a trip – anything that can stop you from over-thinking.

Try new things – learn to play the piano, hug a tree, if that's what works for you, watch a squirrel eating his food, etc. Come out of your comfort zone and break all the barriers. Be open to new relationships – don't raise a wall and shun away people. Go with the flow and give time for new relationships to grow on their own. Don't go investing too much of yourself emotionally. This is not just for partners, but for friends too.

Self-healing is important for you to overcome your emotional wounds, especially after narcissistic abuse. The wound can become fresh and raw if left unattended, which can make you a victim of another narcissistic relationship or rekindle your old abusive relationship. Invest your energy and time in learning about yourself and your behavioral patterns. Understand the characteristics of your narcissistic partner, and use the experiences as a tool to prevent yourself from getting abused again.

Learn to say NO when you are not interested and practice it more fiercely. Connect with your deeper self. Now that you are holding the keys of your life, don't hand it over to anyone else again – however genuine the person is.

Day 16: When its okay to fake it

So you don't feel like there is anything to be cheerful about, I get that. Do this one thing and I promise you would feel better in less than 30 days. Fake it! Fake the bounce in your step, fake the smile when you say hello to your neighbour or co-worker. Fake the dance when your favourite song or any song for that matter comes on the radio.

When I say fake it, I don't mean that it should appear fake. Muster all the energy you have to make it as real as can be. As bad a forced smile sounds, research shows that it will make anyone feel happier. Try activating the smile muscles in your face by smiling and notice how you suddenly feel calmer and happier.

Being cheerful keeps you healthy. It is slow death to be gloomy all the time.

Proverbs 17:22

Prayer: Lord, help me to do everything necessary to regain my Joy. No matter how silly or difficult it might seem. I am depending on you for the will to try.

Day17: Take time to hear from God

Put a priority on hearing form God in this season. He has something to say about your situation that would bring peace into your heart in a way that no one else can do, because he knows you like no one else does. When you pray and meditate on his word, ask him to speak to you, and most importantly, be expectant to hear form him.

When he speaks to you, act on what he has said. Its so funny how two people going to similar problems can pray for a solution and get two completely opposite directions.

Listen to them, people of Israel, and obey them! Then all will go well with you, and you will become a mighty nation and live in that rich and fertile land, just as the LORD, the God of our ancestors, has promised.

Deuteronomy 6:3

Prayer: Father speak to my heart and help me to hear you and obey. Draw me close to yourself as I draw closer to you dear Jesus.

Day18: Surrender

Have you ever tired so hard to get something and even when you tried harder, things only seemed to get more complicated? Those are the times when complete surrender is appropriate. Being a child of God means that we would always be just that- his children.

Like the popular hymn goes 'when all around me is sinking sand, on Christ the solid rock I stand"

I encourage you to totally surrender to Jesus, and let him trade your weakness for his strength. When it seems like the logical thing to do at this time is take control of your life. The one and only thing you need is to surrender it to God.

So that it is no longer I who live, but it is Christ who lives in me. This life that I live now, I live by faith in the Son of God, who loved me and gave his life for me.

Gal2:20

Prayer: Lord, help me to resist the temptation of holding onto control of my life. I surrender all to you, my will, my emotions, my intellect.

Day19: Purpose from pain

Everything that happens to us, can be a stepping stone to greater things. One day, you would be able to turn this pain into a testimony that liberates and helps many people in a similar situation.

He helps us in all our troubles, so that we are able to help others who have all kinds of troubles, using the same help that we ourselves have received from God.

2 Corinthians 1:4

Prayer: Lord, let me be the light that shines on the path for other victims to find their way to freedom, victory and healing.

Day20: The way out

A friend of mine Shawna, was dating a covet Narcissist for over 8 years, the abuse got so bad, she thought she was going crazy. Her self esteem took a bad hit, and she thought she would never be able to find anyone to love her, so she stayed. God can make a way out, no matter how complicated your situation might be. He did it for Shawna.

Every test that you have experienced is the kind that normally comes to people. But God keeps his promise, and he will not allow you to be tested beyond your power to remain firm; at the time you are put to the test, he will give you the strength to endure it, and so provide you with a way out.

Prayer: Father, thank you for giving me the strength to survive emotional abuse. Thank you for showing up at the perfect time and making a way out for me.

Chapter Five: Don't Fall for a Narcissist Again

Reclaiming your mind is the first step you need to do when you are recovering from narcissistic abuse. This is because the insanity of narcissism can consume you completely that you forget the purpose of your life. You will have to start from the scratch – right from claiming your birthright (feeling, thinking and action) to fighting for your individuality. You will need to get back the space (physical, emotional and psychological) you were deprived of. Slowly, but steadily, you get there – you get to know that you are worthy to be loved and there is a reason behind your existence.

All this happens when you begin to heal yourself – it is definitely a long and tiring journey, but it is not impossible. You need to be determined and strong to get back on your own legs. Give time for the wounds to heal – don't rub on to it by revisiting the unpleasant memories.

How Do You Save Yourself from the Radar of a Narcissist?

When you come out of an abusive relationship with a narcissist, you become more vulnerable and can be easily intimidated. You might also end up attracting the wrong person into your life and sometimes this cycle repeats. Why does this happen?

It often takes months or even years to realize that your partner is a narcissist. You don't realize it unless you get into the research mode. When you realize your relationship is turning toxic and consuming your happiness, you begin to look at things from a different perspective. Coming out of the relationship immediately doesn't sound good to you so you give it some time but then, when things get out of control, you have no choice but to walk away.

Good that you did that. You healed and recovered, but what if you are close to repeating the same mistake again? Educating yourself about narcissism and its patterns is crucial, but you should know when to stop. When you start Googling about the symptoms every time you come across a person, you are going to go insane. If you keep thinking about your ex-partner's behavior and keep comparing it with the new relationship, then you are unknowingly attracting the same. Remember the Law of Attraction? Whatever you seek, seeks you.

Don't keep burying the emotions within you. Write a journal. Every time you get triggered by your past, don't suppress your emotions but, instead, write it down. Jot down whatever thoughts you get. Every time your thoughts change towards a particular incident, write it down. Whenever you feel you have an eye-opener, write it down.

For example: You ponder over your past when your ex-partner had said you are worthless and selfish. Even after so many months, you still feel the hurt engulfing you. Instead of getting caught with the emotions, do some reality checks. Think about all the good things that had happened to you. Remind yourself about the number of people who had called you a beautiful soul because of your selfless acts. You will soon realize that the narcissist was actually using the cheapest trick to thrash your self-esteem.

End of a relationship doesn't mean the end of the world. It is a start of a new life. You have already done your exercise of self-educating about narcissism. You will now need to invest time in knowing who you are (especially after the recovery of the abuse as you will not really know you are). Unless you bring back your old self, the old you, it is going to be difficult as you might continue to attract toxic people. Take conscious efforts to revitalize and work on yourself.

Stop thinking that you are unworthy of love because this one thought is enough to go and land yourself again in the hands of a narcissist or abuser. Regardless of how long it is going to take, you need to believe that you are worthy of experiencing love again and live life the way you always wanted to. Don't fall back to negative thoughts and behavioral patterns. Every time you are caught with a negative thought, swap it with a positive thought.

For instance, don't allow the self-defeating thought to engulf you by saying, "My ex-partner never saw anything good in me. What if I was really not good enough? Maybe, I should have worked more on understanding him better? It must have been my fault."

Replace this thought with a self-mastery one, "I did the best I could, but the inefficiency of my ex-partner clouded his mind in seeing it. It isn't my fault anymore. I can't help it if he has a deficit. Never will I allow anyone to ill-treat me again."

"If you change the way you look at things, the things you look at change." – Wayne Dyer.

Day 21: He freely gives

Our human nature is vindictive, hard hearted and driven by personal desire by default. After surviving an abusive relationship, we might become toxic ourselves without knowing it. The Holy spirit living in our hearts makes all the difference. Where we have hate he trades it for love, where we have confusion he brings in clarity.

But the Spirit produces love, joy, peace, patience, kindness, goodness, faithfulness, humility, and self-control. There is no law against such things as these.

Galatians 5:22-23

Prayer: Father let all the fruits of your spirit be made manifest in my life, only you can truly change my heart. Help me to submit to your spirit as he does the good work in me.

Day22: More than you ask for

Your surviving is hinged on your dependence on God. Those who wait on the lord would mount up with wings as eagles. Whatever things you desire, find them in him. God is saying to you through his word, you can be anything. You are limitless, you are blessed.

To him who by means of his power working in us is able to do so much more than we can ever ask for, or even think of

Ephesians 3:20

Prayer: Lord I believe you can make my life much better everyday as I walk with you. Let none of my dreams be lost, help me find and fulfill those great plans you have for me.

Day23: Question Marks

Life is full of mysteries we may never fully understand. Some questions we have would never be answered logically. Why did my marriage fail? How will I get through this? What if I never fully recover? At times, God gives us clear answers to some of these tough questions but not every time. What do we do at such times, we could get angry and give up or we could decide to keep trusting him no matter what. Because we understand that everything he does for us is for our ultimate benefit. We know he loves us so we keep holding onto him.

For I am certain that nothing can separate us from his love: neither death nor life, neither angels nor other heavenly rulers or powers, neither the present nor the future, neither the world above nor the world below—there is nothing in all creation that will ever be able to separate us from the love of God which is ours through Christ Jesus our Lord.

Romans 8: 38-39

Prayer: Father, I lift up every unanswered question in my life over to you. I trust that you know what's best for me. I leave every difficult situation I your powerful hands, do for me what only you can do.

Day24: Guide my way

The path of the righteous shines brighter and brighter. This is my confession today. Old things have passed away. As discussed earlier, try not to focus on what you don't want in your life, rather focus on the qualities you want to see in new relationships. Educate yourself, and continue to learn. Most importantly ask God to give you wisdom to make better decisions in every area of your life.

Your insight and understanding will protect you and prevent you from doing the wrong thing. They will keep you away from people who stir up trouble by what they say

Proverbs 2: 11-12

Prayer: Lord, keep negative people away from me. Let me focus on growth, positivity and as I do so surround me with your presence every step of the way. Grant me insight and understanding to keep me from failing.

Day25: Never Again

This is the last time, that I would have to go through emotional abuse. This affliction would repeat in my life. Henceforth I am walking in the path the lord has set for me. The path that leads to peace, love, righteousness and joy.

The road the righteous travel is like the sunrise, getting brighter and brighter until daylight has come.

Proverbs 4:18

Prayer: Never again Lord. I pray that I would never be a victim of abuse again. I am more than a conqueror. Equip me with everything I need, Thank you for your promises.

Day 26: Pray for your relationships

There might be other people you have hurt while being in a toxic relationship, because you were pressured into cutting them off, or maybe something more complicated that you alone understand. If you can ask for their forgiveness, that would be awesome. But before you do please pray and ask the lord to soften their hearts

Try to be at peace with everyone, and try to live a holy life, because no one will see the Lord without it.

Hebrews 12:14

Prayer: Father, if I have hurt anyone knowingly or unknowingly, please bring it to my knowledge so I can make amends. Soften their hearts towards me and help us find peace and reconciliation.

Day27: Pray for your abuser

I hope all the days of prayer and meditation on the word has prepared your heart for this moment. Narcissistic personality disorder is a disease and they need help as much as you do. So pray for them, that they would also find healing and peace.

"You have heard that it was said, 'Love your friends, hate your enemies.' But now I tell you: love your enemies and pray for those who persecute you, so that you may become the children of your Father in heaven. For he makes his sun to shine on bad and good people alike, and gives rain to those who do good and to those who do evil.

Mathew 5:43-45

Prayer: Father, I commit (insert names) into you hand, father heal them and let them find salvation in you. All things are possible in your name, nothing is too difficult for you. Thank you Lord.

Day28: The real enemy

The real enemy of any child of God is not the abuser or the slandering friend. The real enemy is the devil. His one agenda is to kill, steal and destroy your life. But the bible says we should resist him and he would flee from us. We can do this by drawing close and staying connected to Jesus. The enemy is cunning and he knows that we cannot win any battle on our own so he fights to keep us away from praying and studying the word of God.

Prayer: Father, I can only remain victorious when I stay connected to you. Help me to place you at the center of everything I do. Let me not get so distracted with chasing things that I forget that seeking your kingdom first, adds all other blessings to my life

Day29: Storms will come

God doesn't promise us a life free from trouble, they would still be storms. Relationships would still have challenges as two imperfect people walk together. Emotional and physical storms come, and at such times, we need to hold on to our unshakable father. Find support among friends who are believers is key to overcoming trying times. Gods word would give us peace if we make it the authority we believe.

The mountains and hills may crumble, but my love for you will never end; I will keep forever my promise of peace." So says the LORD who loves you.

Isaiah 54:11

Prayer: Whatever comes my way lord, I commit to you. You will not let me fall, I depend totally on you. Thank you Jesus.

Day30: Thankful

All things are working for my good.

I confess that I am Loved.

I am blessed.

Lines are falling in pleasant places for me.

I will never be ashamed

I am like a tree planted by the water

My life in hidden in Christ.

I am thankful for your saving grace.

Conclusion

We have come to the end of the book. I sincerely hope this book was useful and helped you as a reader to get a clear and in-depth understanding of narcissistic abuse. This book provides information on how to identify narcissistic abuse, how to handle it, the ways to recover from it and the steps you must take to heal.

The chapters will provide the readers with important guidelines on how to protect and shield themselves from being attacked by narcissistic abusers. Most importantly, the prayer and meditation guide after every chapter, would help survivors healing and take them from turmoil to peace as the days go by.

The book has covered the primary objective, which is to act as a complete guide for readers who would like to know in detail about narcissistic abuse.

I sincerely hope this book was useful and you feel better equipped to rebuild and enjoy your life.

Thank you, and best wishes.

Sources

https://www.psychologytoday.com/intl/blog/resolution-not-conflict/201210/are-you-narcissist-6-sure-signs-narcissism

https://www.yourtango.com/2018309713/3-types-narcissists-signs-someone-narcissist

http://flyingmonkeysdenied.com/definition/baiting/

https://www.psychologytoday.com/us/blog/understanding-narcissism/201705/narcissistic-love-patterns-the-romantic

https://medium.com/@SoulGPS/3-steps-to-stop-missing-your-narcissistic-ex-break-the-trauma-bond-and-start-a-new-life-726c5d2dc97a

https://herway.net/life/8-stages-healing-escaping-narcissistic-abuse/

https://letmereach.com/2014/06/14/how-to-stop-attracting-narcissists/

https://www.psychologytoday.com/us/blog/toxic-relationships/201709/how-spot-narcissistic-abuse

https://www.psychologytoday.com/intl/blog/toxic

-relationships/201806/how-handle-narcissistic-abuse

https://narcissistabusesupport.com/stages-of-grief-after-narcissist-abuse/

http://www.howtokillanarcissist.com/narcissistic-abuse-recovery/

https://www.psychologytoday.com/intl/blog/tech-support/201606/why-recovering-the-narcissist-in-your-life-is-so-hard

Printed in Great Britain
by Amazon